Home Ground

Home Ground

Don Gutteridge

First Edition

The John B. Lee
Signature Series

Hidden Brook Press
www.HiddenBrookPress.com
writers@HiddenBrookPress.com

Copyright © 2018 Hidden Brook Press
Copyright © 2018 Don Gutteridge

All rights for poems revert to the author. All rights for book, layout and design remain with Hidden Brook Press. No part of this book may be reproduced except by a reviewer who may quote brief passages in a review. The use of any part of this publication reproduced, transmitted in any form or by any means, electronic, mechanical, photocopied, recorded or otherwise stored in a retrieval system without prior written consent of the publisher is an infringement of the copyright law.

Home Ground
by Don Gutteridge

Cover Image – from a painting by Gerald Parker: Black Lake.
Cover Design – Sol Terlyson Kennedy
Layout and Design – Richard M. Grove

Typeset in Garamond
Printed and bound in Canada
Distributed in USA by Ingram, in Canada by Hidden Brook Distribution

Library and Archives Canada Cataloguing in Publication

Gutteridge, Don, 1937-, author
 Home ground / Don Gutteridge. -- First edition.

Poems.
ISBN 978-1-927725-58-0 (softcover)

 I. Title.

PS8513.U85H56 2018   C811'.54   C2018-903853-5

For Bruce Ashdown:
In Memoriam.

Table of Contents

– Black Lake – *p. 3*

Part One
To the Point

– Ballast – *p. 6*
– Moon Over Monk – *p. 7*
– Cochise – *p. 8*
– Match – *p. 9*
– Wiz – *p. 10*
– Helm – *p. 11*
– Apostasy – *p. 12*
– Our Side – *p. 13*
– Rare – *p. 14*
– Chums – *p. 15*
– Abide – *p. 16*
– Bully – *p. 17*
– Numb – *p. 18*
– Dark – *p. 19*
– Towards the Light – *p. 20*
– Typical – *p. 21*
– Ribsy – *p. 22*
– Pleasure – *p. 23*
– Vain – *p. 24*
– Birthday – *p. 25*
– Two For Grace Leckie – *p. 26*
    – Wraith
    – Afar
– Two For Mrs. Bray – *p. 27*
    – Magical
    – Phalanx

– Some Words – *p. 28*
– Prayer – *p. 29*
– Urge – *p. 30*
– Still – *p. 31*
– Hello, Donald – *p. 32*

Part Two
In The Now

– Endued – *p. 34*
– Stun – *p. 35*
– Walking the Ice – *p. 36*
– Etched – *p. 37*
– Syllables – *p. 38*
– Exuberance – *p. 39*
– Remembrance – *p. 40*
– Bite – *p. 41*
– Myrrh – *p. 42*
– Pincers – *p. 43*
– Cuppa – *p. 44*
– Mother – *p. 45*
– Baltimore – *p. 46*
– Sneeze – *p. 47*
– Sizzle – *p. 48*
– Joy – *p. 49*
– A Blind Man Builds a House – *p. 50*
– Sinister – *p. 51*
– Boost – *p. 52*
– Mutual – *p. 53*
– Gay – *p. 54*
– Migraine – *p. 55*

– Together – *p. 56*
– The Meek – *p. 57*
– Dancer – *p. 58*
– Proud – *p. 59*
– Mariners – *p. 60*
– Humour – *p. 61*
– Thursday – *p. 62*
– Heroic – *p. 63*
– Laureate – *p. 64*
– Man of Parts – *p. 65*
– Next – *p. 66*
– Voice – *p. 67*
– Bench – *p. 68*
– My Turn – *p. 69*
– A Birthday Poem – *p. 70*
– Finesse – *p. 71*
– Defy – *p. 72*

About the Author – *p. 75*

Home Ground

Black Lake

After a painting by Gerald Parker

One alabaster moon
was not enough lustrous
light to lavish on Black
Lake's unruffled,
silvered surface, so you
added a ravishing red
dot above the very
spot where a pair of loons
ululated on the cusp of lust
and the little stream feeding
filigree never slackened
its pace, and just to subvert
the scene you drew a sunny
butterfly fluttering
on monogrammed wings
over the outcrop
where we stopped to wonder
if this was all a dream.

Part One

To the Point

Ballast

I was born in Sarnia (alas)
but was soon rooted fast
in the groomed ground of the Point,
safe in the grasp of grand-
father's lawn, as green
as grass rinsed by rain,
I knew every eave and ell,
every sill and gable,
and I roamed the alleys and by-
ways in search of the me
I ought to be, seeing
with my enviable eye: the River
Flats where our kites flew
like swift-swooping swallows,
the River throbbing like a
struck vein, the Lake
as blue as blue-jay's
bobbing wing, Canatara
where the sand sang in the sun
and thunder rang over
its dune-dense immensity,
the elm-shade as big as a
behemoth's bellyful of umbrellas
and the pine-cones we flung
like gratuitous grenades in our joy
at being here, at knowing
this place lay deep
in the ballast of our bones.

Moon Over Monk

The moon over Monk Street
sits above the horizon
like a serene replica
of Mara's lamp, each
mellowing its light along
the sacred place where we play
our gently gendered games
in embossed luminosity,
like miller-moths thrilled
to be illumed and shadow-
free: we think of Artemis
and her Grecian bow, bent
wise and unneutered
by the night.

Cochise

Whenever my fourth line
friends and I played
cowboys and Indians,
I fought to be the Comanche
with my willowed bow and arrow
and rooster's feather clipped
to my cap (the wild child
inside me aching
to get out), and if
the script demanded it,
I would fake a cinematic
demise, break a territorial
treaty or ululate
against all things
east, and I wonder now
whether those poems
I prized about our home-
grown aboriginals (boosting
them into public view)
had their beginning in those
days when I first essayed
Geronimo or Cochise.

Match

The Reverend Bell came home
one afternoon, flung
his cellar door wide
and, though less than wise,
lit a match: we found him
sitting in a singed patch
of his grass: surprised,
a touch unhinged,
and wondering how such
things come to pass
and whether God was on
his side.

Wiz

For Dave Withers
In Memoriam

If the good die young,
you were its poster-child,
mowed down in your prime,
and you, my boyhood
chum whom we dubbed "Wiz",
were our guide and idol, whose
hands badgered, out of thin
air, gadgets and gizmos
of every ilk, and wood
worked as soothing as silk:
you kept us amused,
and we boasted of just
knowing you, and I wished
you a long and beguiling life,
humming with joy and the fruits
of your wide and wild imagination.

Helm

I might have been five
when I first wandered into
my grandfather's work-
shop, and watched the hands
I loved guide a lozenge
of elm or oak through the burr
and bite of the band-saw,
a particle of the puzzle he was perfecting
piece by filigreed piece,
and I nuzzled in closer,
waiting, in my need, for the pause
that preceded the unspoken
tousling of my cowlick,
and knowing I would be cherished
and thrive here with this
man at the helm.

Apostasy

My grandmother baked
pies on Sunday mornings
(cherry and rhubarb
in season, raisin for my
Grandpa's bucket), an echo
away from the Anglican nave
and apse she had no
reason to give the nod
of approval to nor taste
its soothing pieties, for she put
all of her love and out-
sized ardor into the gentle
kneading of her dough and braving
the wrath of a hairy-jawed
God, while we feasted
on her pastries and praised the Lord

Our Side

My uncle's best and abiding
friend was Ernie Rosenbloom,
and we spent many an early
evening together on Cameron
Lake with a new moon
looming, angling for perch
and the odd large-mouth,
but no one told me
that Ernie had been super-
intendent of the Foundry,
where, at his urging, a gang
of goons with massive bats
broke up a sit-down
strike with soundless fury
and not a twinge of regret,
and sent the Polacks surging
towards their ramshackle
homes, burned to the ground:
instead, I watched Ernie
unhinge the hooks from a doomed
bass's jaw as tenderly
as a grandpa dandling
a tot, and I thought then
that God was always on our
side.

Rare

On rare occasions my grand-
father would march us
to Canatara beach, and while
he squatted alone on the sand
in his Sunday suit, Bob
and I paddled apace in the
fluted shallows, and feeling
perfectly safe in his hands,
we ventured up to our waists
and even dove under
like daring dolphins, while Grandpa
smiled at us and we smiled
back at him: it was only
later we learned that he couldn't
swim.

Chums

Nancy and I were chums,
playing our garrulous games,
gender-free, in Withers
field, festooned with sun-
light in the long summer
afternoons or under
Mara's lamp in the usurping
dark of Monck Street,
superintended by a marinating
moon—until the day
I took a fancy to her burgeoning
beauty and felt my heart
hum and a voice inside
singing Olly, Olly
en-fray.

Abide

My Uncle Potsy and I
go hunting cottontail
in a sun-stunned meadow,
and, if we are lucky, spot
a jackrabbit anteloping
speed in an open field,
but there is this day
no game to be got,
but all I need is striding
side by side with my uncle,
our guns as silent as the thoughts
we share, with a love that abides

Bully

Six-year-old
Susan Coote liked
to ride her trike around
our block, passing my house
en route, and one day
I simply stood my ground,
grasped the handle-bars
and pulled the baffled girl
aside, and I still remember
that infantile incident
and wonder why I became
something I was not:
a bully.

Numb

Coop and I at Canatara,
nude in the change-room,
our young sprouts at attention
as we spot a spy-hole
(hopes a-bloom despite
our doubts) and press ourselves
numb to catch someone
gendered other than us
easing off her one-
piece and showing her un-
mentionable to our prying
eyes, when suddenly
the prize is blotted out
by a well-placed thumb,
without so much
as an if you please.

Dark

When Leckie's field iced
over after a thaw
and quick freeze, we skated
on glazed meadows
where once clover bloomed,
wild mustard throve
and larks buffeted the air –
as if the globe had hewn
one raw rink
where we left in our wake
filigreed meridians,
mittened our hands in gendered
pairs, and unmuffled
our carnal cries – two
abreast lest we fall
off the world: amazing
the moon as we moved through
the lustrous rendering
of its light towards the star-
flecked obsidian dark.

Towards the Light

Nightfall along Monk
Street, Mara's lamp
tossing its amber glow
against the dread of darkness
beyond, we hover
round its blossoming beam
like moths fanning a flame,
and only when the game begins
do we test the inked shadow
where we hide like prey
pursued until the oley
oley en free
releases us, knowing
full well that, like
every living thing,
we all grow towards
the light.

Typical

On a typical July day
with cumulus clouds caressing
the high sky over
Canatara, an unplugged
sun, and a southerly breeze
dusting the dunes dulcet,
we cast an eye towards
the languid-lipped beauties
sanctifying the sand,
and in the lull between waves
we defy the Lord and his blessings
by turning our thoughts to the
luxuries of lust.

Ribsy

We called him Ribsy in gentle
mockery of his mange-ridden
coat and skeletal stare,
this stranger stray
who arrived each day
at noon on the dot to win
dibs on our crusts or the odd
scrap of bologna as we basked
in the autumnal sun on the
school steps, and once
in a while one of the girls
would essay a wary pat
and the grateful dog would wag
a tail or two or give out
a rheumy-eyed grin,
but when the snows came in,
lock, stock and barrel,
Ribsy passed us by,
and we wondered if even
God had taken pity on him
or whether he found a warm
spot to die.

Pleasure

I loved the way the girls
of Canatara lay
their beautiful bodies
belly-down on the hot
sand in long-legged
leisure, and let the sun's
fire play bare-backed
wherever it would,
and I liked to think they
were begging to be perused
by those of us too shy
to stare (our bravado soon
jellied), who welcomed
the Lake's chill upon
our thigh-high desires,
infused still with prurient
pleasure.

Vain

In a vain attempt to bond
my Dad took me
and his thirty-ought-six
to a nearby farm where the gun's
elephantine report
would not disturb the neighbours,
and instructed me on how to be
a rifleman: I pressed
the butt against my shoulder,
aimed at the next tree,
pulled the trigger and found
myself on my own butt,
stunned and flat on my fanny,
the tree unharmed,
and it dawned on me then
that bonding was no trifling
matter.

Birthday

When, as a boy, I lay
in Sarnia General with a temperature
of a hundred and four
and the nurses poured sulfa
drugs into the midst of my fever,
I thought only of the pain
engulfing me, and when
I awoke next morning
sweatless, I wondered if I had
a date with the future or any
say in its slow unfolding,
but the story told itself,
the tale of a life lived
with little regret, way-
laid by joy and surprised
to be turning eighty.

Two For Grace Leckie

Wraith

You were a face in my dreams,
a blue-eyed wraith
apostrophized by a pair of
pigtails, with a smile
that would have set the sun's
beaming afire, and when
I am wakened, abrupt as a blink,
you are as far away
as an archipelago of stars,
and I must do with
two rows over
in a callow country school
bereft of your budding grace:
faithful as ever to the march
of my blood's desire.

Afar

Romeo had a balcony between
him and juvenile Juliet
and I too loved
from afar: two rows
over where I could see
you luminous in the lickerish light
of the school windows, your perfect
profile leaving me to fret
while you dallied and beguiled
or squeezed a glancing eye
in my direction, your smile
a gift I would remember
romancing all the way
home.

Two For Mrs. Bray

Magical

Mrs. Bray's magical
house floated on flowers,
doused to the sills with bloom,
and we watched her dote on her
groomed garden, arrayed
in roses and poppies and rimmed
by hollyhocks with only
the brim of her floppy hat
showing, and we thought of the
shock of widowhood,
which she bore like a badge.

Phalanx

When Granny Reeve died,
I remember the golden
gladioli from Mrs. Bray's
groomed garden and a casket
buried in bloom from her pied
bower, which seemed to ease
our grieving, and I thought
of Granny being carried
to Heaven on a phalanx
of flowers.

Some Words

I remember my grandmother
whispering, "He died of a stroke,
poor man," and instantly
I conjured hammer blows
cracking a skull as the victim
gasped his last breath,
his loved ones keening,
but then I had another
thought: perhaps it was a tender
thumb caressing the flesh
to death: some words
say more than their meaning

Prayer

"If I should die before
I wake, I pray the Lord
my soul to take" was my nightly
prayer when I still believed,
when Heaven still had heft
and God did not deceive
in one of his many disguises,
but when I am gone,
I'll be remembered in the loving
eyes of my children and grand-
children, and when they too
have passed and what is left
of the measure of their memory,
perhaps I'll still have a word
or two to say in the pith
of a poem or the startle of a story,
as long as there are ravenous
readers to treasure them:
perhaps the world will not
forsake me after all,
if I should die before
I wake.

Urge

When I began to scribble
poems and stories at the age
of twelve, I had to delve
into my daylight dreams,
where the point of all plots
and the insurgencies of rhythms
lay waiting to be beamed
abroad beside those
images I liberated
from my impious imagination:
the motive for metaphor runs
deep: we are steeped in the
simple home-truths
of our youth and the unstoppable
urge to write.

Still

How many times was I
awakened by your lyrical babble
just down the hallway,
how many Sunday mornings
did we spend dabbling
in Duplo, in the playroom
we built for the two of us,
how many hours did we spend
fishing in Cameron and its blue
brilliance? How many days
did we spend on holidays
in far-off places
like quaint Quebec or Ottawa,
mottled by museums: you
were a gift from a compassionate
god, our dearest wish
come true: you were always
aloft in our thoughts, and still
are.

Hello, Donald

At the Point's sesquicentennial
celebration, I found
my Aunt Betty, looking
very much her age (after
an absence of three years)
in the crowd watching the town's
new fire engine
breeze by in a blaze
of scarlet: "He's over in the fire
hall looking at old
photos," she said, so I crossed
the street and entered the fire
station, where, at rows
of long tables, a crush
was peering at vintage snaps;
I squeezed in beside an elderly
gentleman, his eyes
on the memorabilia in front
of him: somewhat tall,
a little stooped but one
who had once been an athlete;
it was then that my Uncle Potsy
turned to me and said:
"Hello, Donald."

Part Two

In The Now

Endued

For Anne

When you pulled up
in that brand-new
Volkswagon with the sun
roof, my heartbeat
abrupted, as the girl with the
clementine curls, a smile
festooned with freckles and a
glance that rhymed with romance
stepped into the autumnal light
in her lemon-yellow dress
and I was smitten breathless,
bitten by love's bite,
and needed no proof
for my endued delight or
my sublime obsession.

Stun

In your lemon-yellow dress
you stun the sun and the
fellow gazing at you
debouching from your Volks-
mobile unfazed
and effortless in your element,
and I fell in love with those
irradiant eyes just
for the fun of it, I must
confess, knowing my heart
could feel no other
wise and hoping some
day you would return
the favour, vouchsafing
our mutual union.

Walking the Ice

I wonder what it's like
to come to the edge of everything,
to walk out on a ledge
of ice with only the bare
blue of the frigid lake
to greet you, a decision
to be made in the nick
of a second, voices urging
"Do it!" and all those
dark trickling days
behind, surging one
farther into the darkness that refuses
to let go? Before
some wee instinct
inside, a voice not otherwise
heard announces the fight
to be, that there is
enough light to slake
the thirst for something
final and other: a living
on, a giving in to life's
uncalamitous cycle,
a carrying on, distinct
and true

Etched

In this birthday drawing
by Tom (which has pride
of place in my study): the two
of us angling for "Rockies"
or any other piscatory poacher
tempted to broach our bait,
and sitting in my uncle's boat
with our lines dangling over
the side in the weeds Tom
has scrawled in bold green
strokes, and I am distinguished
by a folksy black beard,
while my grandson
guides the motor he has sketched
with admirable accuracy,
and above it all three-
storied brown clouds
and an orange sun blooming
like a Christmas chrysanthemum,
etched with love

Syllables
For John B. Lee

We started a conversation
about poems and their making,
about the inheld breath
before we say the syllables
to ourselves and dream
them onto the page,
willing some meaning
that seems beyond knowing,
some home-truth
that needs no proof
to startle the world we build
together in a friendship
welded by words.

Exuberance

For Bruce Ashdown: In Memoriam

Everything you did was out-
size, you galvanized gumption,
you put the imp in impish,
you spun yarns about
the track and all its magical
mystique like a riffling raconteur,
welcomed with a nod and a wink,
you could scan a racing form
like a blind man brushing
braille, you struck a racquetball
as if it were Hitler's head,
your golf stroke was a whiff
and two slashes, you manoeuvred
your skiff with sails set
as close to the wind as audacity
allows, your hand on the tiller
as supple as a lover's touch,
you had a heart as big as a
thoroughbred's, the blood-
lines you admired more than
the life you lived with such
endued exuberance.

Remembrance
For My Grandfather, In Loving Memory

Did you hear the sonorous
soaring of the Last Post
over your country's memorial,
the bugle singing as sadly
sweet as Gabriel's music
commemorating the brave in their
quiet graves, or the roaring
of the jets in salubrious salute?
Did you, my gloried grandfather,
come awake at such
concatenation, recall
your days doleful in that
far-away war?
No longer feel forsaken
by the souls you fought so
valiantly to save? Be
assured, we will remember,
though Time itself flies,
until the Earth un-
endures and the sun dies.

Bite

Being a loner himself,
it never occurred to God
that Adam might be lonely,
but seeing it so
He created woman to be
his constant companion, and made
her curves and contours
as pleasing as possible, for there
was the issue of issue, should
the need arise, for even
the flowers had bees to buzz
from pod to pistil like
helicopters on helium and each
ripened apple dropped its seed
into the dappled shade below,
and thus all was well
and the cherubim wished Him
Godspeed, until Eve,
to spite her Maker, took
one blistering bite.

Myrrh

Christmas 2017

When Gabriel's horn awakened
shepherds on the high hills
above Bethlehem, they hearkened
to the Heavenly news and followed
it under a star-stippled
sky to the stable where the Babe
lay lovingly in a manger's
hay, feeling blessed
to be born, while further
East, Magi, forsaking all,
moved mountains to bring
Him frankincense and myrrh,
while lambs purred in animal
amazement and cattle lowed,
stunned in their stanchions, and far
away the Earth lurched
an inch towards Eternity.

Pincers

My Dad on skates: as quick
as Rocket Richard with the grace
of Gordie Howe, he skimmed
the ice with nary a pause
for the applause that rocked
against the rafters,
he stick-handled with the ease
and breakaway speed
of a whirling dervish,
and with a pride that brimmed
beyond the rink, un-
furled against the world:
I worshipped his every
magical move, but me:
my blades sagged ankleward,
and all I had to offer
as penance were my ink-stiff
stanzas and stilted stories,
but, even though
I knew my failure rankled,
I was sure that someday
since he left me bereft
I would capture that gifted glory
in the pincers of a poem.

Cuppa

Ever since whenever
Anne and Claire have met
for coffee and innocent
chatter: the forgivable
foibles of friends and neighbours,
the pettiness of politicians,
the puffery of princes,
the entitlements of the rich
and privileged few, world
events that really matter –
all wrapped up
in a cuppa or two: the kind
of ritual that keeps the conversation
going, pertinent and prime,
that makes our collaborations
civil, and seals friendship
for a lifetime.

Mother

My mother lacked the maternal
touch, but she made up
for it by trying harder:
she had my baby photo
tinted and formally framed
(I keep it proudly on the wall),
I remember picnics in Canatara,
the seven months she nursed
me through rheumatic fever
without a hint of complaint,
and trips to Clyde Beatty's
Circus, where she clapped
louder than the lions, she played
rap rummy like a pro,
and I can see her on hands
and knees scrubbing the kitchen
floor or hear her listening
to "I Love a Mystery"
on the radio: she's been dead
these forty-five
long years, but my memory
of her is still radiant.

Baltimore

In the tallest tree an oriole
trills in the morning with a
song like the low, throaty
notes of a diva aereating
her aria, and I strain to see
that black and orange blur
brush the breeze (its black
inkier than onyx and orange
that would shame a day-lily),
and when he deigns to visit
our feeder and sift our sugar
syrup, we feel the thrum
of the natural world in all
its humbling glory, and in the
hush of evening we hearken
to the Baltimores saying
goodnight to each
other with a final chee-
cheer-up.

Sneeze

Penning poems can be
a bit of a tight-rope
trick: words balanced
on the brink of meaning,
import that must be
teased out syllable
by syllable before they ink
the page with their passionate
purpose: composing is a
high-wire trapeze
act (nothing to be
sneezed at.)

Sizzle

For Tom

And so here we are
once again talking
books on a June afternoon:
under your gentle questioning
and encouraging looks
I probe the private precincts
of my memory for details
about my pentameters and plots
with forays into family
stories I share for the first
time: of long lost
grandfathers and a forgotten
war and killing ground
where no birds trilled,
and we are drawn to one
another in the succinct silences
of our caring conversation
by the sizzling wizardry
of words.

Joy

And me lugging a film
and audiotape from school
to school like a failed door-
to-door salesman
making his pitch, practicing
his ploy – hoping to prompt
verse out of twelve-year-
olds, peering out
at me and my equipment
with eyes lit up
with an innocence I envy,
and when the film stops,
there is a subtle moment
of silence before the pens
start scratching and I breathe
again as one boy
plugs away at his maiden
poem, hatched from something
itching inside, where words
and joy collide.

A Blind Man Builds a House

For Stan Burfield

Remembering the hours spent
tinkering with Leggo blocks,
the way they welded together
with a satisfying tug,
and you thumbing the tumbled
shapes they made, and then
there was your neighbour's
doll-house, feathering
your fingertips over
its ells and angles, its pitched
gables, its rain-proof
windows, and so it was
you had the basics of a
blueprint and ventured
to build a house of your devising:
bricks laid side
by side, levelled by touch,
recall and the inner eyes
of your imagination, until
your pulsing digits went numb,
with the roof still looming
above you, now alone
with your pride in a vast vacancy
you couldn't fathom even in your
monochromatic dreams –
the last challenge, whose triangular
contours you sensed like embers
in the memory-bank of your mind,
but you were merely blind
enough to find a way
to hammer out a home
you could call your own.

Sinister

My Uncle Tom and I
swung from the sinister side
and patrolled the Thames Valley
fairways in tight tandem,
and while I irritated my irons
with random rambunctions,
his wedge struck his ball
aloft and we watched it
in feathered flight as it
gravitated to the green and, with a
blissful bounce, nestled
there: now golf is a
companionable game of crisp
clicks and sun-softened
putts, and all was well
until the day Tom took
up tennis and forgot he was
fifty-eight: his heart
split like a Christmas walnut.

Boost

My mother's Dad may
have been third generation
Canadian, but he was Irish
to the bone, and no sheep
herder he, but a master
craftsman, a calligrapher
in wood and stone, who dandled
me, September's child,
on his good knee and boosted
me high in his carpenter's
arms, his wild days
long past (without,
I'm told, reneging an ounce
of Gaelic charm), until
that terrible June day
when he was thoughtlessly
murdered, alone in the
moonlight above a
bootlegger's roost,
and so it was that he
became the grandfather
I never got to know
or love.

Mutual

My grandson and I
go manoeuvring down
memory lane: me
to the village that gave me
verve and volume to beam
my voice abroad, Tom
to the place he pictured
from an overdose of my poems
and stories; I point with pride
to this dream-haunted house
or that side street
where one of my creations might have
wandered through my fervid
prose, or to Mara's lamp,
where Nancy first took
my fancy or Foster's pond
where we fleeted on blades over ice
or Withers' field where our games
began and the world ended:
Tom and I cherish this
chance to bond, sharing
these defining moments
when our mutual imaginations
meet and intertwine..

Gay

For my Brother, in Memoriam

The signs were there from the beginning:
you favoured the girl's games
of hopscotch and Double
Dutch and the company of their
velvet voices, their tendrill'd
touch, you eschewed the rough
and tumble of rugby or shinny
on Foster's pond or innings
in Withers' field, you were fond
of Garry with his effeminate
flutter and the two of you
played dress-up
in Gran's cast-offs
with fancy bonnets and spiked
heels (I can still hear
their stiff stutter on our
neighbourhood walk),
and I can't imagine the pain
you must have felt holding
inside some truth
you only half understood
and did not date to utter –
O how you must have longed
to be the being you were meant
to be, while I stood by,
thinking only of me,
complacent in my ignorance.

Migraine

It must be like the pain
Cain felt when the brand
struck his brow, there is
something biblical
about it: our very veins
bludgeoned with blood ex-
plodding in the brain and behind
the throbbing eyes, as if the body
were gripped whole by a vise,
and it even hurts to think,
as we do about Christ rendered
mute on His anguished cross
or Samson at Gaza pulling
down with his bare hands
the pagan temple to ease
the ache no heavenly
supplication can emend.

Together

In this photo, my mother
and father, standing tall
on my grandfather's lawn
in the their Sunday suits,
hold me up high
between them for the camera's
loving eye, like a prized
doll for all the world
to see, their hands tethered
to steady me on my maiden
shoot, as happy as they
will ever be, and I still
regret I wasn't enough
to keep them together.

The Meek

Good Friday: 2017

Today is like any other
except for the sorrow in the
air as that image
of bleak Golgotha rises
unhallowed in the mind:
two thieves and a rebel
mystic pinioned on crosses,
seared by a galvanizing sun,
their sweat swept aside
by the galling winds, while
weeping mothers pray
for quick death, and one
of the crucified, almost
bereft of breath, gives
birth to a final cry:
"O Lord, how can it be
that the meek shall inherit
the Earth?".

Dancer

For Katie

You float across the stage
as light as a breeze breathing
on a feather, your limbs
lissoming fanciful
filigrees as graceful
as a swan silvering a silken
pond, your tapered toe
tethered to the floor, on which
you twirl and pose prettily:
I am your grandfather,
and you a girl of whom
I am particularly fond:
for me you are both
the dancer and the dance.

Proud

For Tom

We've always been proud of you:
even as a toddler you showed
us your sweet temperament,
and as a lad you gentled horses
at Circle-R and led
your charges with devotion
and esprit de corps, and we
remember the mirth you brought
us on the teen-age stage
and how you let your eyes
seek pleasure in the world
of books and the treasury
of their poems and stories, and what
a vet you've been, the embodiment
of courage and care and wise
beyond your years: let
the all-seeing Earth
entreat your belonging
and shout out loud
its joy at your being.

Mariners

For Bruce Ashdown, In Memoriam

We set sail for Chantry,
tacking all the way
against a southerly breeze:
you at the tiller guiding
us tactfully with the ease
of a sea-going skipper,
while we, the crew, provide
the necessary ballast,
and when at last we reach
that fabled isle, you cry,
"At least we'll ride the wind
home," but when the sun
purples in the west, the wind
slackens and dies, so that
skipper, crew and the un-
buffeted boat, fore,
aft and bow, have to be
paddled and purred north-
ward to French Bay,
where the wives applaud
such paralyzing prowess,
safe on the luff-free
shore.

Humour

In this dream, my sister
and I are scrapping (I have
no sister but dreams
seldom lie) hurling
insults, near blows,
our words bent with anger,
when my Dad, hearing
rumours from the next room
of our roughhousing, comes
in and pulls us apart,
and me, still enraged,
cry, "Put 'em up!"
and Dad raises his dukes,
ready to engage, before
he grins and slowly lowers
his fists, and the dream ends,
reminding me of what
I liked most about
my father: toughness
gentled by a sense of humour.

Thursday

For Ken Cooper

Every Thursday for more
years than we wish to count,
we gathered with our gang at
Hickory Ridge and scrambled
our way around its measured
meadows: I see you still
with your sawed-off swing
and a ball-flight that sang
in the buoyant breeze, while I
whittled and walloped,
happy to amble among
such cheerful companions
and to treasure the memories
that bridge the gap between
then and the seasons to come.

Heroic

All I have left of my father
is this plaque from the
Cosy Café for some
long-forgotten feat,
but it is enough to set
me imagining my Dad
on skates with stride-strong
strokes as smooth as a
swan flows over
the perfect parabola of a pond,
or like some winged Icarus
seducing the sun, the rink
his royal residence, while
townsfolk cheer
his every dipsy-doodle
deke and dodge, his heroic
brio, and I wonder now
if he dreamed me fondly
amid all the hullabaloo,
and did he know it would take
a war and thirty years
drink to keep us apart
and leave me heart-bereft.

Laureate

For John B. Lee

You are the poet laureate
of laureates, a farm boy
harvesting hay and silaging
corn, while words rose
out of the fallow as easily
as a bard's breathing and tantalized
with the possibilities of joy
and sorrow, and, unlaurelled,
you surprised yourself
with poems, stooked with extravagant
stanzas, encharmed by rapturous
rhythms and metaphors
that would move a misanthrope,
you gazed deep into your rural
roots and the hibiscus of our
history with a soul hopeful
of humanity: you smote the Muse
and wrote.

Man of Parts

For John Ogletree

It must be nice to be
at home in your own skin,
even when the body it suffers
occasionally betrays it:
you are a scion of science
who travelled the world just
to see what it had to say,
an aficianado of the outdoors,
of bird-breathing fields
and trunkless tundra mirroring
the sky's aqua look,
you took up golf at sixty
and struck the ball as if
it mattered, you tell a droll
tale with an twinkling eye,
you put the friend in friendly,
you are a patron of the arts,
of poetry inked in love
and pied plays: suffice
it to say you are a man
of parts no poem
can fully extol.

Next

I wish with all my might
there was a Heaven, a palatial
place where I might greet
all those who have allowed
Death to inconvenience
their lives, and where we would thank
the Lord for having had
the good sense to save
our breath for the right religion
and to have avoided six
of the Seven Deadly Sins
and find our grace in God's
sanctified text:
and when our smiles have faded,
we, unjaded,
will wonder what to do
next.

Voice

For George Martell

A voice on the phone: warm,
inspiring confidence,
urging me to begin
our friendly intellectual
chatter: the left view
your humane choice, me
slightly on the right, we feed
at the marketplace of ideas
in the comfort of companionship;
I can't believe you've agreed
to go, leaving me alone
with my scattered thoughts, grieving
for a man who's lived his life
as if it mattered.

Bench

For Doug McConnell, In Memoriam

When one of our own is wrenched
suddenly from us, we do
our best to memorialize
him in poem or song
or a simple dedicated
bench on the course where his out-
size drives seasoned
the air above its manicured
meadows and all his putts
dimpled the cup: whenever
we sit there now
to reflect in the unqualified
quiet on the reasons why,
a little bit of Doug
resides beside us.

My Turn

Whenever I think of death,
I take a deep breath
and congratulate myself
on being alive, ever
since that day
long ago when I wished
my way out of the womb and uttered
my first articulate cry
and wondered how many
had come before me
in humanity's slow bloom
all the way back to the
great apes and their generous
genes and the dinosaurs who groomed
the ancient foliage of the Earth
and finally the fish-churned
sea where something
grew anew, a birth
with no antecedent,
a blip in God's thought,
and here I am against
the odds still living,
waiting patiently for my turn.

A Birthday Poem

For Anne

We have stopped counting
our birthdays, but the years
glide on without permission
or our say-so, but we have eased
into our age as gracefully
as Time and Earth allow
(your hand in my glove),
and whatever fears
we may have for the future
are flouted by our abiding love.

Finesse

For Isabel Huggan

You were a writer before
you learned to write: plots
rose up in your toddler's
mind: fables in their infancy,
nursery rhymes re-rhymed,
images bobbling for some-
thing to fertilize their fancy,
and when the first syllables
rolled unhobbled
onto the pencilled page,
the stories you'd hoarded so
long, burst onto
the world's stage, cobbled
crisp: character caressed
by craft, scenes finessed
with ease, humanity distilled
in the fierce piercing of words

Defy
For Stan Burfield

For more than a dozen years
you were surrounded by blooms
in your shop, a long way
from Alberta's unlyrical
land, and when you tried
your hand at verse, were
your first poems for poppies
and their roaring red, sonnets
for sunflowers a-burst
in lavish light, haiku
for hibiscus and their passionate
purple, or pentameters
for peonies and their kissing cousins?
Did you let them speak
for you, go soaring through the
petrified petal of your fear?
For poetry is both bliss
and consolation, a way of speaking
to the world that subsumes
both shy and defy.

About the Author

Don Gutteridge is the author of more than fifty-five books: poetry, fiction and scholarly works in educational theory and practice. He was born in Sarnia, Ontario and raised in the nearby village of Point Edward. He graduated from Western with an Honours English degree, taught school for seven years and then joined Western's Faculty of Education. There he taught English methods for twenty-five years and is now Professor Emeritus. He won the 1972 UWO President's Medal for the best periodical poem of that year, "Death At Quebec." His poetry collection *Coppermine* was short-listed for the 1973 Governor General's Literary Award. To listen to interviews with the author, go to: http://thereandthen.podbean.com. Don lives in London, Ontario with his wife Anne.

www.ingramcontent.com/pod-product-compliance
Lightning Source LLC
LaVergne TN
LVHW090036080526
838202LV00046B/3841